Contents

Colour: Prakash S. and C. Ramesh **Special Text:** Sanjana Kapur and Aparna Kapur

Special Illustrations: Adarsh Achari and Ritoparna Hazra **Assistant Colourist:** Silambarasan K.

Layout: Sivajith S. **Cover:** Arijit Dutta Chowdhury **Art Director:** Savio Mascarenhas

Editor : Reena Ittyerah Puri

JATAYU

MANY STORIES ARE TOLD ABOUT THE GREAT VULTURE, JATAYU. HE WAS THE SON OF ARUNA, THE SUN GOD'S CHARIOTEER, AND HE WAS THE NEPHEW OF GARUDA, THE MOUNT OF VISHNU. HE WAS A BIRD OF MAJESTIC PROPORTIONS, AND WHEN HE SPREAD HIS WINGS, IT SEEMED AS THOUGH THEY COVERED THE WHOLE SKY.

JATAYU LIVED WITH HIS OLDER BROTHER, THE MAGNIFICENT SAMPATI WHO WAS THE KING OF BIRDS, IN A DEEP FOREST FULL OF TALL TREES AND WONDROUS CREATURES.

EVEN AS HATCHLINGS, BOTH THE BROTHERS HAD BEEN FOND OF FLYING AT DIZZYING HEIGHTS, CHALLENGING THEMSELVES AND EACH OTHER.

LET'S SEE WHO REACHES THAT PEAK FIRST!

AS THEY GREW OLDER AND STRONGER, THEIR RACES BECAME MORE FREQUENT AND DANGER-RIDDEN.

SLOW DOWN, JATAYU!

I CAN SEE THE WHOLE WORLD FROM UP HERE!

THEY WOULD OFTEN FLY UP TO MEET THEIR FATHER, ARUNA.

ARUNA, YOU MUST TELL YOUR SONS NOT TO FLY SO CLOSE TO US UNLESS THEY WANT TO BE SCORCHED.

I WILL, MY LORD.

MY SONS, YOU MUST NOT COME NEAR US.

IT'S DANGEROUS.

DON'T WORRY ABOUT US, FATHER.

ARUNA'S ADVICE WENT UNHEEDED.

THE TWO BROTHERS ROSE HIGHER AND HIGHER, THEIR WINGS BEATING FASTER THAN EVEN THE WIND.

OUR FOREST LOOKS LIKE A SPECK OF DUST FROM UP HERE.

SUDDENLY –

I'M STARTING TO FEEL A LITTLE TIRED. BUT I'VE FLOWN GREATER DISTANCES BEFORE WITHOUT A MOMENT OF FATIGUE. I WONDER IF SAMPATI'S FEELING THE SAME... NO, HE SEEMS TO BE ALL RIGHT.

JATAYU IS GAINING SPEED! ON THE OTHER HAND, I FEEL QUITE TIRED AND BREATHLESS. AT THIS RATE, I WON'T BE ABLE TO STAY AHEAD OF HIM FOR MUCH LONGER.

SOON –

IT'S BLAZING HOT! WHERE ARE WE? MY THROAT IS PARCHED. EVERY INCH OF MY BODY SEEMS TO BE ON FIRE. MY BROTHER LOOKS EXHAUSTED TOO. WHAT IS HAPPENING TO US?

IT WAS SAMPATI WHO REALISED WHAT WAS WRONG.

WE ARE TOO CLOSE TO SURYA! IT MUST BE NOON NOW. NO WONDER THE SUN GOD IS SHINING SO BRIGHTLY.

THE GREAT BIRD WAS FILLED WITH PANIC.

I CAN HEAR THE SOUND OF SURYA'S HORSES.

THE CHARIOT WILL BE HERE ANY MOMENT... IT'S TOO LATE TO FLY AWAY... WE'LL BE BURNT TO DEATH!

IF I STOP THE CHARIOT, THE UNIVERSE WILL BE THROWN OUT OF BALANCE AND THERE WILL BE UTTER HAVOC.

MY SONS... OH NO!

I MUST CONTINUE ON MY PATH. FORGIVE ME, MY CHILDREN.

UNAWARE OF THE IMMINENT DANGER, JATAYU WAS STILL INCHING TOWARDS THE SUN.

JATAYU, NO!

OH, HOW DO I SAVE HIM?

SURYA'S CHARIOT WAS DANGEROUSLY CLOSE NOW.

THERE'S ONLY ONE WAY....

WITH A FINAL BURST OF SPEED...

...SAMPATI FLEW OVER JATAYU, STRETCHING HIS WINGS WIDE TO SHIELD HIS BELOVED BROTHER.

THE FLAMES ATE UP SAMPATI'S WINGS, AND HE HURTLED TO THE GROUND IN PAIN, HAVING LOST THE POWER OF FLIGHT.

AAAAAAGH....

SAMPATI! NO!

SAMPATI, MY BRAVE SON! WHAT A GREAT SACRIFICE YOU HAVE MADE!

JATAYU ALSO FELL, EXHAUSTED AND BROKEN.

SAMPATI, WHERE ARE YOU?

SAMPATI HAD FALLEN ON MOUNT MAHENDRA, WHERE –

I AM UNABLE TO MOVE... AND THE PAIN... IT IS UNBEARABLE.

LET ME TEND TO YOUR BURNS.

SAMPATI REMAINED THERE FOR THE REST OF HIS DAYS, UNDER THE CARE OF THE KIND SAGE NISHAKARA. THE TWO BROTHERS NEVER MET AGAIN.

MANY YEARS LATER, IN THE KINGDOM OF MITHILA –

WHAT A BEAUTIFUL COUPLE THEY MAKE! YOU WILL AGREE WITH ME, KING DASHARATHA.

YOU ARE RIGHT, KING JANAKA.

RAMA, THE ELDEST SON OF KING DASHARATHA OF AYODHYA, WAS GETTING MARRIED TO SITA, THE DAUGHTER OF KING JANAKA OF MITHILA.

THE WEDDING PROCESSION REACHED AYODHYA WITH MUCH POMP AND GAIETY. DASHARATHA'S THREE WIVES WELCOMED SITA WARMLY.

SOON –

I HEREBY PROCLAIM MY ELDEST SON, RAMA, AS THE PRINCE REGENT OF AYODHYA.

THE WHOLE KINGDOM REJOICED AT THE NEWS...

...EXCEPT FOR ONE PERSON – MANTHARA, A MAID IN THE PALACE. SHE POISONED THE MIND OF KAIKEYI, RAMA'S STEPMOTHER.

HOW CAN YOU SIT SILENT, O QUEEN? YOUR SON, BHARATA, SHOULD BE THE KING. DEMAND YOUR RIGHTS!

AND SO –

MY KING, A LONG TIME AGO, YOU GRANTED ME TWO BOONS WHEN I SAVED YOUR LIFE IN THE BATTLE AGAINST THE ASURAS.

I WANT YOU TO GRANT THOSE BOONS TO ME NOW.

WHAT DO YOU WANT, KAIKEYI? I WILL NOT REFUSE YOU ANYTHING.

NAME OUR SON BHARATA AS YOUR HEIR, AND SEND RAMA INTO EXILE FOR 14 YEARS.

WHAT ARE YOU SAYING? HOW CAN YOU ASK SUCH A THING OF ME?

KAIKEYI REMAINED ADAMANT.

FATHER, I CANNOT LET YOU BREAK YOUR PROMISE. BHARATA IS AS WORTHY OF THE THRONE AS I AM.

I WILL DO AS MOTHER WISHES AND GO INTO EXILE.

MY PLACE IS BY YOUR SIDE.

SO IS MINE, BROTHER.

AND SO –

PRINCE RAMA, WE WILL FOLLOW YOU TO THE FOREST.

NO, MY PEOPLE. YOU MUST REMAIN IN AYODHYA.

MY CHILDREN BANISHED!

UNABLE TO BEAR THE SEPARATION, DASHARATHA SOON PASSED AWAY.

RAMA, LAKSHMANA AND SITA WERE INFORMED BY BHARATA ABOUT THE TRAGEDY.

RAMA CONTINUED IN HIS EXILE, AND THE THREE TRAVELLED DEEP INTO THE PANCHAVATI FOREST.

ONE DAY –

I HAVE NEVER SEEN A BIRD OF SUCH GIGANTIC PROPORTIONS.

WHY, IT'S AS BIG AS A HILLOCK!

BEWARE, BROTHER! IT COULD BE A RAKSHASA IN THE GUISE OF A VULTURE.

DO NOT BE AFRAID. MY NAME IS JATAYU. YOU MUST BE THE SONS OF DASHARATHA... YOU LOOK SO MUCH LIKE HIM.

YOU KNEW OUR FATHER?

OH YES! WE WERE DEAR FRIENDS.

TELL ME, HOW IS HE?

OUR FATHER IS NO MORE.

RAMA TOLD JATAYU THE STORY OF THEIR EXILE FROM AYODHYA.

12

I CANNOT BELIEVE MY DEAR FRIEND IS GONE.

IF ONLY I COULD HAVE MET HIM ONE LAST TIME.

TELL US HOW YOU MET OUR FATHER, GREAT BIRD.

JATAYU TOLD THEM THE STORY.

A LONG TIME AGO, A FEARSOME DROUGHT STRUCK AYODHYA.

THE RAINS HAVE FAILED US. THERE WILL BE NO HARVEST THIS YEAR.

HOW WILL WE FEED OUR CHILDREN?

JUST A LITTLE MORE RICE, MOTHER.

NO, WE HAVE TO SAVE A MOUTHFUL FOR YOUR FATHER.

O KING, OUR CHILDREN ARE STARVING. SAVE US FROM THIS TERRIBLE FAMINE!

I PROMISE YOU, I WILL FIND A WAY.

"DASHARATHA CONSULTED THE ROYAL PRIESTS.

WHY ARE WE BEING PUNISHED LIKE THIS? HAVE I OFFENDED SOME GOD?

LORD SHANI'S EVIL EYE IS UPON AYODHYA.

THEN I WILL FLY TO THE HEAVENS AND SEEK SHANI OUT. I WILL BEG HIM TO PUT AN END TO OUR SUFFERING.

YOU MUST BE VERY CAREFUL, YOUR MAJESTY.

IF LORD SHANI'S EYE FALLS ON YOU, YOU WILL BE KILLED.

"DASHARATHA SET OUT.

"SHANI SENSED DASHARATHA APPROACHING HIM.

DASHARATHA IS COMING TO MEET ME! I CANNOT LET HIM GET CLOSE TO ME. I PROMISED BRAHMA I WOULD NOT CAST MY EYE ON ANY LIVING CREATURE.

THERE HE IS!

"SHANI FLEW FASTER.

HE'S EVADING ME. BUT I CANNOT GIVE UP. MY KINGDOM IS AT STAKE.

"I WAS WATCHING THE CHASE FROM A DISTANCE.

THAT'S DASHARATHA, THE KING OF AYODHYA CHASING SHANI! IT WILL SURELY GET HIM INTO TROUBLE. LET ME HELP HIM.

I'M GETTING CLOSER.

HE'S STILL FOLLOWING ME! I HAVE TO STOP HIM.

"I MANAGED TO CATCH YOUR FATHER AS HE FELL.

YOU ARE SAFE NOW.

WHO ARE YOU, O GREAT BIRD?

MY NAME IS JATAYU. I AM THE BROTHER OF SAMPATI, THE KING OF BIRDS, AND THE SON OF ARUNA, THE SUN GOD'S CHARIOTEER.

MY UNCLE IS GARUDA, THE MOUNT OF VISHNU.

I'M INDEBTED TO YOU FOR LIFE.

I HAVE HEARD MANY STORIES ABOUT YOUR COURAGE AND WISDOM, DASHARATHA. I COULD NOT HAVE LET YOU PLUMMET TO YOUR DEATH.

BUT TELL ME, O KING, WHY WERE YOU CHASING SHANI?

MY KINGDOM HAS BEEN STRUCK BY A GREAT FAMINE. MY PEOPLE ARE STARVING. IT IS ALL BECAUSE SHANI'S EVIL EYE IS UPON AYODHYA.

DASHARATHA, YOU ALMOST LOST YOUR LIFE PURSUING SHANI. YOUR CHARIOT IS IN FLAMES. CLIMB ON TO MY BACK, AND I WILL TAKE YOU HOME.

HOW CAN I GO BACK TO AYODHYA, HAVING FAILED IN MY TASK?

JUST THEN –

I HAVE NEVER WITNESSED SUCH VALOUR. I PROMISE YOU, AYODHYA WILL NOT SUFFER ANYMORE.

SHANI DEV!

I THANK YOU, LORD.

HAIL KING DASHARATHA! HE HAS SAVED US FROM DEATH!

I MUST BID YOU FAREWELL NOW, BUT I GIVE YOU MY WORD, I WILL COME TO YOUR AID WHENEVER YOU NEED ME.

THANK YOU, NOBLE FRIEND!

I PROMISED DASHARATHA THAT I WILL ALWAYS BE THERE FOR HIM AND HIS FAMILY AS LONG AS I HAVE BREATH IN MY BODY. YOU DO NOT HAVE ANYTHING TO FEAR IN THIS FOREST.

WE ARE GRATEFUL TO YOU, JATAYU.

LAKSHMANA BUILT A SIMPLE HUT CLOSE BY WHERE THE THREE COULD STAY.

ONE DAY, WHEN RAMA AND LAKSHMANA WERE OUT –

WILL YOU GIVE ME SOMETHING TO EAT?

YES, OF COURSE, REVERED SIR.

BUT –

HA HA! YOU ARE MINE NOW!

NO! LET ME GO!

IT WAS RAVANA, THE DEMON KING OF LANKA, IN DISGUISE.

DRAGGING SITA INTO HIS CHARIOT, RAVANA TOOK OFF INTO THE SKIES.

HELP! SOMEBODY, PLEASE SAVE ME!

THAT'S SITA'S VOICE!

JATAYU ATTACKED RAVANA, FIGHTING BRAVELY WITH ALL HIS MIGHT.

AAAAAARGH!

BUT SOON –

I AM LOSING MY STRENGTH. MY LIMBS ARE FAILING ME. RAVANA IS TOO POWERFUL, AND I HAVE BECOME WEAK WITH AGE.

HA HA! YOU FOOLISH THING! YOU MAY BE A MIGHTY BIRD, BUT YOU ARE NO MATCH FOR ME.

NO! PLEASE DON'T HARM HIM.

DEAF TO HER PLEAS, RAVANA SLASHED AT JATAYU WITHOUT MERCY.

MY WING!

MEANWHILE –

SITA...

SITA! WHERE ARE YOU?

SOMETHING HAS HAPPENED. SHE MUST HAVE BEEN TAKEN AWAY BY FORCE.

SHE CAN'T BE VERY FAR AWAY. LET'S GO LOOK FOR HER IN THE FOREST.

SITA!

DO NOT DESPAIR, BROTHER. WE WILL FIND HER, EVEN IF IT MEANS TAKING HEAVEN AND EARTH APART.

AFTER A WHILE –

LOOK, ISN'T THAT JATAYU ON THE GROUND? HE'S TERRIBLY WOUNDED!

JATAYU! WHAT HAPPENED? WHO DID THIS TO YOU?

FORGIVE ME, RAMA. I TRIED MY BEST TO SAVE SITA. BUT HE WAS TOO POWERFUL FOR ME....

WHO WAS IT?

R...RAVANA. HE CUT OFF MY WINGS AND TALONS.

I'M USELESS WITHOUT THEM.

OH JATAYU! YOU PUT YOUR OWN LIFE IN DANGER TO SAVE SITA.

YOU MUST GO NOW... RESCUE SITA FROM THAT EVIL DEMON'S CLUTCHES.

THEY WENT SOUTH.

JATAYU HAD HELD ON FOR THAT LONG ONLY SO HE COULD TELL RAMA WHAT HAD HAPPENED. NOW THAT HIS WORK WAS DONE, JATAYU BREATHED HIS LAST.

WE WERE NOT ABLE TO PERFORM THE LAST RITES FOR OUR FATHER, BUT WE WILL GIVE JATAYU THAT HONOUR.

YOU ARE RIGHT, BROTHER.

THE TWO BROTHERS BUILT A PYRE OUT OF FRAGRANT WOOD FOR THE GREAT BIRD.

I WILL BRING THE WATER OF THE SEVEN SACRED RIVERS.

WATER FROM THE RIVERS SPRANG UP FROM THE SPOT WHERE RAMA'S ARROW PIERCED THE GROUND AND JATAYU'S SOUL WAS GRANTED SALVATION.

SAGE SHILADA WAS IN DEEP MEDITATION. HE HAD BEEN PRAYING TO SHIVA FOR MANY YEARS.

FINALLY, EARLY ONE MORNING –

WHAT DO YOU WANT, SHILADA?

O SHIVA, I LONG FOR A CHILD.

YOU WILL GET WHAT YOU DESIRE.

CONTENT AND HAPPY, SHILADA RETURNED TO HIS ASHRAM.

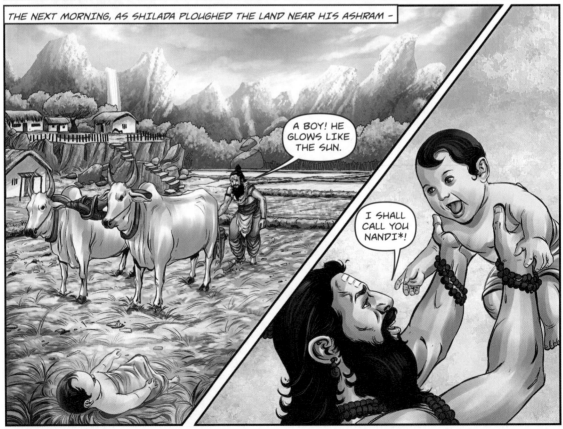

THE NEXT MORNING, AS SHILADA PLOUGHED THE LAND NEAR HIS ASHRAM –

A BOY! HE GLOWS LIKE THE SUN.

I SHALL CALL YOU NANDI*!

*ONE WHO BRINGS JOY

28

THE SAGES HAD A COMFORTABLE STAY. AFTER A FEW DAYS –

IT IS TIME FOR US TO LEAVE NOW.

MAY YOU LIVE A LONG AND PROSPEROUS LIFE, SHILADA.

IT HAS BEEN AN HONOUR SERVING YOU.

MAY YOU ALWAYS BE HAPPY, NANDI.

SAYING THIS, THE SAGES LEFT.

AS THE SAGES WERE WALKING AWAY –

WHAT IS THE MATTER, SHILADA?

PLEASE STOP!

WHY DIDN'T YOU BLESS MY SON WITH A LONG LIFE?

BECAUSE... WE COULDN'T.

YOUR SON DOES NOT HAVE LONG TO LIVE.

WE ARE SORRY.

SHILADA RETURNED HOME, HEARTBROKEN.

WHAT IS WRONG, FATHER? YOU LOOK SAD.

NOTHING, MY SON.

TELL ME, FATHER. WHAT IS WRONG?

OH MY SON! THOSE SAGES, MITRA AND VARUNA, SAID THAT YOU....

SHILADA TOLD NANDI WHAT THE SAGES HAD FORESEEN.

IS THAT ALL? WHY ARE YOU SO WORRIED?

YOU TOLD ME THAT LORD SHIVA WATCHES OVER US.

HOW CAN YOU BE AFRAID? HE WON'T LET ANYTHING HAPPEN TO US. I'LL PRAY TO HIM.

MAY YOU BE VICTORIOUS, MY SON.

NANDI ASKED FOR THE SAME BOON YEAR AFTER YEAR. HIS DEVOTION TO SHIVA WAS UNBREAKABLE.

AFTER A FEW YEARS –

OPEN YOUR EYES, NANDI. YOU DO NOT NEED TO DO THIS ANY MORE.

YOU ARE ALREADY IMMORTAL. ASK FOR ANYTHING.

ALL I WISH IS TO BE AT YOUR SIDE FOR EVER.

SO BE IT. YOU WILL BE MY VEHICLE AND MY CLOSEST AIDE.

SHIVA BLESSED NANDI, TRANSFORMING THE BOY INTO A DIVINE BULL.

HE TOOK NANDI TO HIS HOME ON MOUNT KAILASH.

SHIVA TRAVELLED ON NANDI WHEREVER HE WENT.

ONCE, WHEN THE GODS AND THE ASURAS CHURNED THE OCEAN TO OBTAIN THE LIFE-GIVING AMRITA...

...A DEADLY POISON SPEWED OUT, THREATENING TO ENGULF THE WORLD.

IT IS HALAHALA!

WE ARE DOOMED!

THE GODS PLEADED WITH SHIVA.

PLEASE SAVE THE WORLD, O LORD.

I WILL DRINK ALL THE POISON. COME, THERE ISN'T A MOMENT TO LOSE.

LOOK! THE POISON IS SPREADING THROUGH THE WORLD. HURRY, NANDI!

SHIVA BEGAN DRINKING THE POISON.

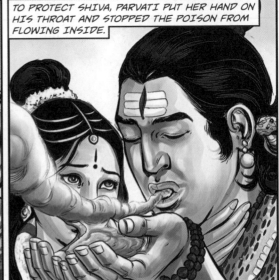

TO PROTECT SHIVA, PARVATI PUT HER HAND ON HIS THROAT AND STOPPED THE POISON FROM FLOWING INSIDE.

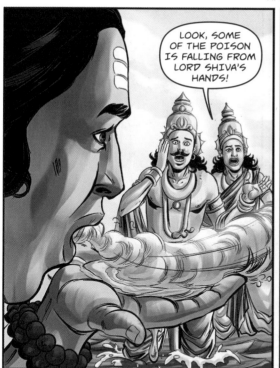

LOOK, SOME OF THE POISON IS FALLING FROM LORD SHIVA'S HANDS!

IF THAT POISON FALLS ON THE GROUND IT COULD KILL THOUSANDS. I MUST DO SOMETHING.

NANDI TURNED HIS HEAD AND –

OH NO! NANDI IS DRINKING THE POISON! IT WILL DESTROY HIM!

BUT –

IT HASN'T HARMED HIM AT ALL! WHAT A WONDER!

NANDI'S DEVOTION TO SHIVA WAS PRAISED THROUGH THE THREE WORLDS.

ONE DAY, RAVANA, THE TEN-HEADED KING OF LANKA, CAME KNOCKING AT THE GATES OF SHIVA'S ABODE. NANDI WAS GUARDING IT AS USUAL.

STOP!

HOW DARE YOU COME IN MY WAY? NO ONE STOPS THE MIGHTY RAVANA.

LORD SHIVA AND MOTHER PARVATI ARE NOT TO BE DISTURBED.

YOU CANNOT ENTER, WHOEVER YOU MAY BE.

YOU CANNOT STOP ME. OUT OF MY WAY, YOU INSOLENT MONKEY!

NANDI WAS ENRAGED.

YOU FOOL! HOW DARE YOU INSULT ME!

YOUR ARROGANCE WILL BE YOUR END.

YOU WILL ONE DAY BE DEFEATED BY MONKEYS.

RAVANA WAS SHOCKED AND RETURNED TO LANKA.

NANDI'S CURSE CAME TO PASS WHEN AN ARMY OF MONKEYS LED BY THE PRINCE OF AYODHYA, RAMA, DEFEATED RAVANA AND HIS MIGHTY ARMY.

IT IS SAID THAT NANDI TAUGHT HANUMAN THE HYMNS TO PRAISE SHIVA.

EVERY SHIVA TEMPLE HAS A STATUE OF NANDI DIRECTLY IN FRONT OF THE MAIN SANCTUM SANCTORUM*. NANDI SITS THERE GUARDING HIS LORD THROUGH ETERNITY.

*THE SACRED SPACE IN A PLACE OF WORSHIP WHERE THE IDOL, OR SYMBOL, OF THE DEITY IS PLACED

Uchhaisravas

The pure white, seven-headed horse, Uchhaisravas, was among the gifts that emerged when the devas and asuras churned the Ocean of Milk. This beautiful horse was immediately taken by Indra and became one of his vahanas or carriers.

Once King Revanta, Surya's son, wanted to visit Vishnu and Lakshmi. Being a friend of Indra's, he borrowed Uchhaisravas to travel to Vaikuntha. Lakshmi was so excited to see her brother Uchhaisravas (both were born from the Ocean of Milk) that she was distracted and did not hear something Vishnu said. Annoyed, Vishnu cursed Lakshmi to be born as a mare. Lakshmi tearfully apologised and Vishnu softened. He said that she would return to Vaikuntha after giving birth to a son as glorious as Vishnu himself.

As a mare on earth, Lakshmi prayed to Shiva for a thousand years to find out who the father of this glorious son would be. Finally, Shiva and Parvati appeared, and assured her that they would find a solution. Shiva then sent Vishnu down to earth as a horse to be with Lakshmi. A baby boy was born after which Lakshmi and Vishnu returned to Vaikuntha. The boy was adopted by King Satajit and named Ekavira. He was also called Hehaya, meaning 'born from a horse', and became one of the founders of the Hehaya dynasty.

SHYAMA AND SABALA

ALL THE GODS WERE IN INDRA'S COURT DISCUSSING THE STATE OF THE WORLD, WHEN SUDDENLY –

LORD INDRA, THERE'S A MATTER THAT NEEDS YOUR ATTENTION.

A GROUP OF ASURAS CALLED THE KALAKANJAS WERE TRYING TO GET TO HEAVEN.

SMELL OUR TRIUMPH! WE HAVE FOUND A PATH TO HEAVEN.

WE WILL BUILD AN ALTAR ALL THE WAY UP TO INDRA'S KINGDOM! BRING THE BRICKS AND LET EACH ONE OF US LAY ONE BRICK UPON THE OTHER.

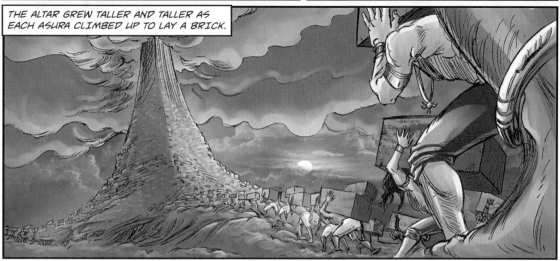

THE ALTAR GREW TALLER AND TALLER AS EACH ASURA CLIMBED UP TO LAY A BRICK.

THE GODS, MEANWHILE, HAD BEEN TRYING TO THINK OF A WAY TO STOP THE ASURAS.

THEIR STRUCTURE IS GETTING TALLER TOO QUICKLY. WE HAVE TO DO SOMETHING, LORD INDRA.

WE HAVE TO FIGHT THEM.

IS THERE A WAY TO AVOID WAR?

I NEED TO TAKE A CLOSER LOOK AT WHAT THEY ARE BUILDING.

INDRA DISGUISED HIMSELF AND WENT DOWN TO SEE.

AS HE WATCHED THE ASURAS AT WORK, HE CAME UP WITH A PLAN.

HE PICKED UP A BRICK AND PLACED IT ON THE ALTAR.

I HOPE THIS WORKS.

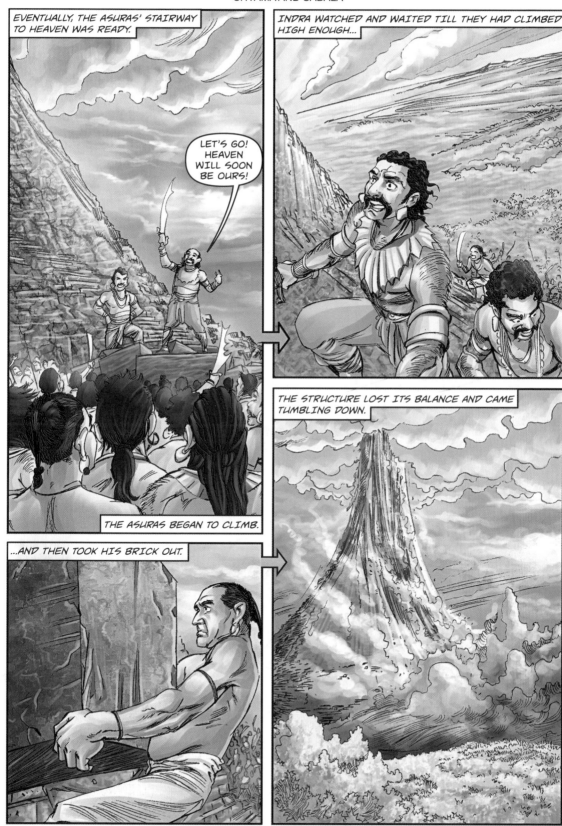

EVENTUALLY, THE ASURAS' STAIRWAY TO HEAVEN WAS READY.

LET'S GO! HEAVEN WILL SOON BE OURS!

THE ASURAS BEGAN TO CLIMB.

...AND THEN TOOK HIS BRICK OUT.

INDRA WATCHED AND WAITED TILL THEY HAD CLIMBED HIGH ENOUGH...

THE STRUCTURE LOST ITS BALANCE AND CAME TUMBLING DOWN.

AS THEY FELL TOWARDS THE GROUND, THE ASURAS STARTED TURNING INTO SPIDERS, AND LANDED SAFELY.

THE TWO ASURAS, WHO WERE ALMOST AT THE TOP, TURNED INTO DOGS.

THEY CAME TO BE KNOWN AS SHYAMA AND SABALA, REPRESENTING DUSK AND DAWN.

YOU WILL GUARD THE GATES OF YAMA FOR ALL ETERNITY.

AND SO, IT IS SAID, THEY DO TO THIS DAY.

AIRAVATA

BEFORE EARTH EXISTED, THERE WAS ENDLESS WATER.

AND OUT OF THIS EXPANSE, A GOLDEN EGG CAME INTO BEING.

THE EGG SPLIT AND BRAHMA, THE CREATOR OF THE UNIVERSE, EMERGED FROM IT.

BRAHMA CREATED HEAVEN AND THE EARTH, WEATHER AND TIME...

...AND CREATURES OF ALL SIZES AND COLOURS.

AMONG THEM, WERE SIXTEEN MAJESTIC WINGED ELEPHANTS, EIGHT FEMALE AND EIGHT MALE. ONE OF THEM WAS THE MIGHTY AIRAVATA, WHOM BRAHMA DECLARED LEADER OF ALL ELEPHANTS.

BRAHMA DECREED THAT AIRAVATA AND ABHRAMU WOULD GUARD THE EAST WITH INDRA. THE SOUTH-EAST WOULD BE GUARDED BY PUNDARIKA AND KAPILA WITH AGNI, AND THE SOUTH BY VAMANA AND PINGALA WITH YAMA.

THE SOUTH-WEST HAD KUMUDA AND ANUPAMA WITH SURYA, THE WEST HAD ANJANA AND ANJANAA WITH VARUNA, AND THE NORTH-WEST HAD PUSHPADANTA AND SHUBHADANTI WITH VAYU.

THE ELEPHANTS WERE SENT IN PAIRS TO EIGHT GODS. TOGETHER, THEY WATCHED OVER THE EIGHT DIRECTIONS.

THE NORTH HAD SARVABHAUMA AND TAMRAKARNA WITH KUBERA, AND THE NORTH-EAST HAD SUPRATIKA AND ANJANAVATI WITH SOMA.

THEY HELPED FORM THE RAIN CLOUDS. THEY ROAMED THE SKIES AND WERE A SYMBOL OF PROSPERITY.

ONE DAY, THE VENERABLE SAGE, DIRGHATAPAS, WAS SITTING IN THE SHADE OF A LARGE VATA* TREE AND MEDITATING.

OMMMM....

AN ELEPHANT HAPPENED TO PASS OVERHEAD.

I'M TIRED. I'LL REST ON THAT TREE FOR A WHILE.

BUT —

C-R-E-A-K

*BANYAN

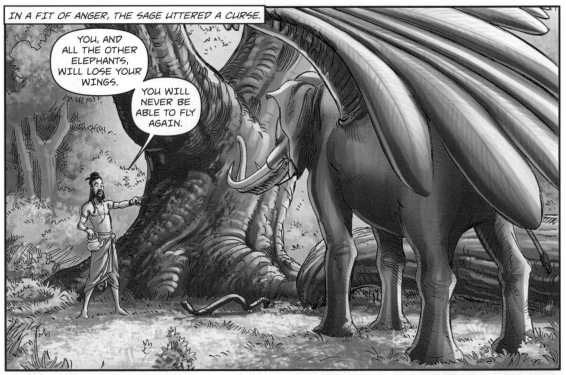

IN A FIT OF ANGER, THE SAGE UTTERED A CURSE.

YOU, AND ALL THE OTHER ELEPHANTS, WILL LOSE YOUR WINGS.

YOU WILL NEVER BE ABLE TO FLY AGAIN.

AND SO IT CAME TO BE, THAT ELEPHANTS BEGAN TO LIVE IN FORESTS.

THE ONLY ONE WHO WAS SPARED FROM THE CURSE WAS AIRAVATA, THE FOUR-TUSKED MOUNT OF INDRA.

IN TIME, INDRA CAME TO DEPEND ON AIRAVATA.

FOLLOW THAT ASURA, AIRAVATA. HE IS GETTING AWAY.

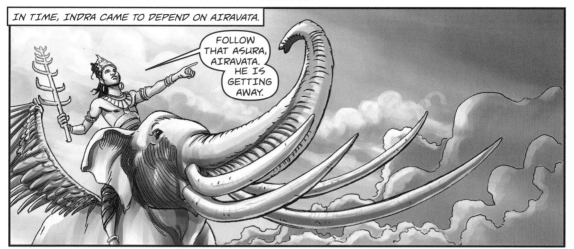

AIRAVATA TOO BECAME FIERCELY LOYAL NOT ONLY TO INDRA, BUT TO HIS FAMILY, AND ALL OF DEVALOKA.

ONCE, THE GODS WERE ATTACKED BY AN ASURA CALLED SURAPADMA.

CHARGE!

SURAPADMA, HAVING EARLIER RECEIVED A BOON FROM SHIVA, COULD NOT BE KILLED.

THE DEVAS FOUGHT WITH ALL THEIR MIGHT BUT THE ASURA ARMY WAS STRONGER.

THERE ARE TOO MANY OF THEM!

THE GODS WATCHED IN DESPAIR.

AS THE BATTLE RAGED ON, INDRA REALISED THAT SACHI, HIS WIFE, WAS THE TARGET.

SURAPADMA IS AFTER SACHI. I WILL TAKE HER AND GO AWAY. AIRAVATA WILL STAY HERE AND HELP YOU ALL.

WITHOUT THEIR KING, THE GODS WERE CONFUSED. THEY LOOKED TO THEIR GURU, BRIHASPATI, FOR ADVICE.

THERE IS NO ONE TO LEAD US. WHAT ARE OUR ORDERS?

JAYANTA, YOU WILL LEAD THE ARMY NOW.

I WON'T LET YOU DOWN.

JAYANTA WAS INDRA'S SON.

ON THE NEXT DAY OF BATTLE, JAYANTA WAS UNSTOPPABLE.

HIS HEROICS DREW SURAPADMA'S ATTENTION.

JAYANTA IS CREATING MAYHEM. I WILL DEAL WITH HIM MYSELF.

HIS ARROW STRUCK JAYANTA DOWN.

AIRAVATA, WHO WAS ALSO IN THE THICK OF THE BATTLE...

...STOPPED FIGHTING WHEN HE SAW JAYANTA FALL.

HE CHARGED ANGRILY AT SURAPADMA'S CHARIOT...

...AND BROKE IT INTO PIECES.

HE THEN TURNED ON SURAPADMA.

SURAPADMA STRUCK BACK...

...AND CUT TWO OF AIRAVATA'S TUSKS.

THEN HE THREW AIRAVATA TO THE EARTH BELOW.

SEVERAL YEARS PASSED. SURAPADMA'S ARMY CONTINUED TO TERRORISE THE GODS.

FINALLY, IT WAS PARVATI AND SHIVA'S SON, KARTTIKEYA, WHO CONFRONTED SURAPADMA.

YOUR PATH OF DESTRUCTION IS AT ITS END.

THE BATTLE WAS NOT EASY.

A BOY LIKE YOU CAN'T DEFEAT ME! GIVE UP NOW.

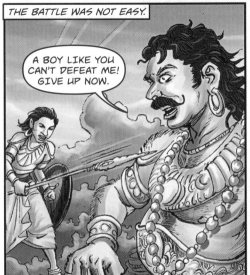

SURAPADMA BEGAN CHANGING HIS FORM TO ESCAPE KARTTIKEYA'S ATTACKS. HE TURNED INTO A BIRD...

...AND THEN INTO A TREE.

THAT WAS A GRAVE MISTAKE, MY FRIEND

KARTTIKEYA SPLIT THE TREE DOWN THE MIDDLE.

ONE HALF OF THE TREE BECAME A ROOSTER, AND THE OTHER HALF BECAME A PEACOCK.

I WILL PLACE YOU ON MY BANNER, ROOSTER.

AND, PEACOCK, YOU WILL BE MY VEHICLE.

...FINALLY OPENED HIS EYES.

AIRAVATA, WHO HAD BEEN UNCONSCIOUS ALL THIS TIME...

LOST AND DEFEATED, HE DECIDED TO PRAY TO SHIVA.

AND SO BEGAN AIRAVATA'S ARDENT WORSHIP.

IMPRESSED BY HIS DEVOTION, AND TOUCHED BY HIS PLIGHT, SHIVA APPEARED BEFORE AIRAVATA.

OPEN YOUR EYES, AIRAVATA.

YOU CAN ASK ME FOR ANYTHING.

LORD, GIVE ME BACK MY PLACE IN HEAVEN.

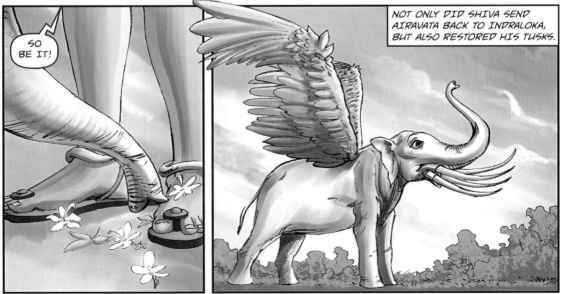

SO BE IT!

NOT ONLY DID SHIVA SEND AIRAVATA BACK TO INDRALOKA, BUT ALSO RESTORED HIS TUSKS.

Airavata

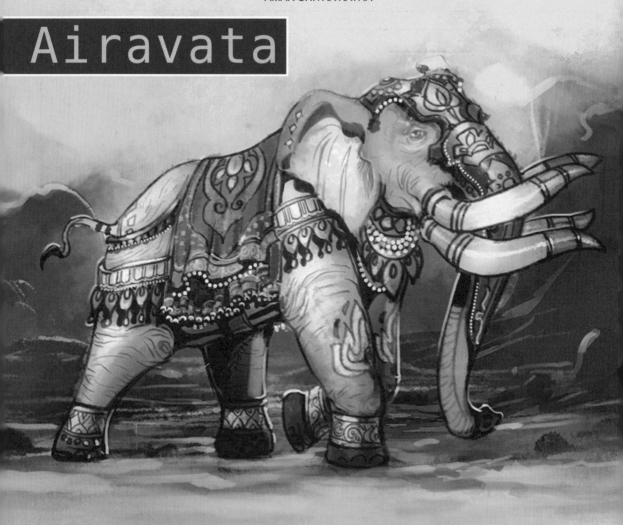

The story in which sixteen elephants emerge from the golden egg is just one version of Airavata's birth. According to the Puranas, Airavata was born to Iravati, a descendant of Kasyapa. On the other hand, *Mahabharata's Adi Parva* describes Airavata as being one of the gifts that emerged during the churning of the Ocean of Milk. In this version, although Airavata was born from Iravati, he went into the Ocean of Milk before it was churned and re-emerged during the churning, gaining his white colour in the process.

Another legend says that Airavata helps the rain god by taking water from the oceans and seas and giving it to the clouds, so that it can then be dispersed by Indra as rain.

GANDABERUNDA AND SHARABHA

THE EVIL KING HIRANYAKASHAPU HAD JUST BEEN SLAIN BY VISHNU'S FOURTH INCARNATION, NARASIMHA.

HIRANYAKASHAPU HAD ONCE ASKED BRAHMA FOR A BOON TO MAKE HIM INVINCIBLE.

I WISH THAT NO MAN OR BEAST BE ABLE TO SLAY ME, THAT I BE IMMORTAL DURING DAY AND NIGHT AND THAT NO WEAPON BE STRONG ENOUGH TO KILL ME.

SO BE IT.

VISHNU'S FORM WAS NEITHER MAN NOR BEAST. NARASIMHA HAD KILLED HIRANYAKASHAPU WITH HIS CLAWS AT DUSK, THUS FINDING A WAY AROUND BRAHMA'S BOON...

...AND RIDDING THE WORLD OF THE EVIL KING'S TYRANNY.

BUT THE TASTE OF HIRANYAKASHAPU'S BLOOD MADE NARASIMHA LOSE SIGHT OF HIS TRUE PURPOSE.

HE CONTINUED KILLING, CAUSING FEAR IN EVERYONE AROUND HIM.

ROAR!

WE MUST STOP NARASIMHA. HE WILL DESTROY EVERYTHING IF HE CONTINUES LIKE THIS!

I WILL STOP HIM.

SHIVA TOOK THE FORM OF SHARABHA, A HALF-BIRD, HALF-LION BEING...

...AND APPROACHED NARASIMHA.

HIS RAGE WILL BE DIFFICULT TO CONTROL.

I WILL ENVELOP HIM IN MY WINGS TO CALM HIM DOWN.

BUT THE ACT ANGERED NARASIMHA.

ARRRRGH!

AND FROM HIS BODY EMERGED A CREATURE, BIGGER AND MORE FEARSOME THAN SHARABHA.

GANDABERUNDA, THE TWO-HEADED BIRD, MET SHARABHA IN BATTLE.

THEY FOUGHT FOR EIGHTEEN DAYS.

THE GODS WATCHED IN HORROR AS THE FIGHT DESTROYED EVERYTHING IN ITS WAKE.

AT THE END OF THE EIGHTEENTH DAY, GANDABERUNDA STOPPED TO LOOK AROUND HIM.

WHAT HAVE WE DONE! EVERYTHING AROUND US HAS BEEN REDUCED TO ASHES. THIS MUST END NOW.

HE SPLIT INTO TWO.

A CALM AND PEACEFUL VISHNU EMERGED FROM THE CENTRE OF THE FEARSOME BEAST.

AT THIS, SHIVA TOO RESUMED HIS FORM.

LET US GO BACK, MY FRIEND.

YES, LET'S.

PEACE WAS FINALLY RESTORED.

Gandaberunda

Gandaberunda, the two-headed bird of unimaginable strength, sits majestically as the official emblem of the Government of Karnataka. Before the Karnataka government adopted Gandaberunda, the mighty bird was the royal insignia of the Wodeyars, a dynasty that ruled the kingdom of Mysore from 1399 to 1947. Images of this mythical bird have been found carved on the walls of the Chennakeshava temple in Belur, and on coins belonging to the Vijayanagara empire. Gandaberunda is often depicted holding an elephant in each of its talons and is said to signify royalty and power.

In another version of the story, it was Sharabha, and not Gandaberunda, who lost sight of his true mission and started destroying everything in his wake. Narasimha was then forced to take the form of Gandaberunda to curb the chaos Sharabha was causing.

Navagunjara

This fascinating mythical being finds its mention in Oriya folklore based on the *Mahabharata*. It is believed that once when Arjuna was out hunting, he came across a creature beyond his imagination. It was made up of nine animals! This magnificent creature had the head of a rooster, the neck of a peacock, the hump of a bull, the waist of a lion, legs of a human, an elephant, a deer and a tiger, and with a snake as its tail. Though initially frightened of Navagunjara, Arjuna soon realised that such a being could only be a manifestation of the divine. Arjuna laid down his weapons and saluted the wondrous creature.

Vahanas - Companions of the Gods

Durga and her tiger

The gods in Indian mythology have vahanas or vehicles on which they ride. These vahanas are their constant companions. They represent the strength and beauty of the deity and at times symbolise various concepts including those that are negative. The negative concepts are those that the gods are said to ride on and overpower.

The more known among the gods and their companions are Vishnu and Garuda, Shiva and Nandi, Brahma and Hamsa, Indra and Airavata, and Ganesha and Moushika.

Durga travels on a fierce tiger.

With a pot of water in her hand, **Yamuna** is depicted riding a tortoise.

Saraswati rides a swan. It is said that she rode an elephant to Shiva and Parvati's wedding.

Yamuna on her tortoise

The **Ashwini Kumaras** are said to ride horses. Though the *Rig Veda* also mentions the donkey as their vehicle.

Kama and his wife, **Rati**, have the parrot as their vahana. Rati is sometimes shown riding a pigeon.

Ganga is said to ride Makara, a creature with the body of a crocodile and the trunk of an elephant.

Ganga on Makara

Varuna on Jaladhi

Varuna's vahana, Jaladhi, was born from Rudra's earwax and has the divine power of movement.

Shani rides a crow. It is said that feeding crows is a way to please Shani.

Surya rides a chariot drawn by seven white horses.

Lakshmi rides an owl. Sometimes, she also rides an elephant.

Kaalratri on her donkey

Kaalratri, a form of Kali, rides a donkey.

Vayu, the wind god, is depicted riding a deer.

Paundraka, the black buffalo ridden by Yama, was born from Rudra's thigh.

The god of wealth **Kubera's** vahana is a man.

Agni, the fire god, rides a ram.

Lakshmi on Uluka

69

Ananta

Kashyapa, one of Brahma's prajapatis, had two wives, Vinata and Kadru. Vinata gave birth to Garuda, and Kadru became the mother of all snakes or Nagas, including Takshaka, Vasuki and Ananta. One day, an argument broke out between Vinata and Kadru over the colour of Airavata's tail. While Vinata insisted that Airavata's tail was pure white, Kadru said that the tail had a few black hairs. (Another version says the argument took place regarding Uchhaisravas' tail.) A wager was placed between Vinata and Kadru to determine the truth. The loser would become the slave of the other for the rest of her life.

Kadru did not want to lose. She went to her serpent sons and told them to suspend themselves from Airavata's tail so it would look like the elephant had black hair. Ananta and a few others refused to be part of this dishonest act. Enraged at the disobedience of her sons, Kadru cursed them. She said that they would die in King Janmejeya's snake sacrifice. Perturbed by his mother's curse, Ananta sought help from Brahma. Brahma told him to go to the netherworld and support Mother Earth on his hood. Ananta readily agreed.

The mighty snake carries the entire world on his hood, maintaining its balance! Ananta is also known as Sheshnag. Vishnu is said to rest on his mighty coils.

Kamadhenu

Kamadhenu is the caring and majestic mother of all cattle in the world. Once, on seeing how hard her children on earth were being made to work, she wept with sorrow. Indra saw her weeping and asked her what the matter was. She told him that her children were being beaten and overworked, which caused her great pain.

Touched by her sorrow, Indra commanded the heavens to open and the rain to fall. It poured for days and the water made it impossible for the fields to be ploughed. As a result, Kamadhenu's children got some much-needed rest.

Kamadhenu is said to live in Goloka, a place above heaven, earth and the netherworld. This special abode was given to her by Brahma.

Amar Chitra Katha's

EXCITING STORY CATEGORIES, ONE AMAZING DESTINATION.

From the episodes of Mahabharata to the wit of Birbal,
from the valour of Shivaji to the teachings of Tagore,
from the adventures of Pratapan to the tales of Ruskin Bond –
Amar Chitra Katha stories span across different genres to get you the best of literature.